CALICO JACK OF THE BLACK FLAG

BY

ANTHONY DAY

Published by Columbine Pictures Press

Copyright © 2017 Anthony Day and Columbine Pictures Press

All rights reserved.

ISBN: 0995555664
ISBN-13: **978-0995555662**

VOLUME ONE

THE CARIBBEAN'S NEW GOVERNOR

AND

THE NEW BOY READ.

DEDICATION

For Stewart,
a short book and a fun read.

1

The sea was calm, the sky was blue without a cloud in view, the wind was light, but still filled the sails, as the English brigantine, The Jill, made her way northward, sailing past the Cay Sal bank, a small group of sandy uninhabited islands, between Florida, Cuba and the Bahamas. The Jill's captain, on seeing Cay Sal's thick forest of palm trees waving in the breeze, knew that it was time to set a new course.

He was a week out of Kingston, having followed the coast of Cuba, and soon he would be in port, adding more products like maize to his sugar and rum before heading back to Bristol.

So, as he strode along his quarterdeck, his Helm at the wheel keeping them straight and steady, nearby his Quartermaster watching the crew working away on the main deck, the Captain was very pleased with himself, as it was days like this which made him glad to be a merchant sailor for the 'Wigglesworth and Grimethorpe Caribbean Trading Company'.

He took his telescope out of his coat's long pocket and opened it out to study Cay Sal. They would have to give it a wide berth, as there was a sand reef several yards out and he knew of a couple of captains who, their ships heavily laden, had come too close and had had to jettison some of their cargo to get free. Though the company treated him fairly, paying a decent wage he and his family could just about live on, losing a few hundred pounds of cargo, he reminded himself, wasn't the best way to make a healthy profit, especially if it was sugar and rum.

'How long now before we reach Miami?' he asked, as he closed his telescope again.

'Four days, Captain,' the Quartermaster replied.

'Good.' He turned to his Quartermaster. 'We'll pick up some barrels of salted fish, and then up to Richmond for cotton to fill our hold, then with all this rum and sugar, it's back to dear old Blighty.'

'Sail, port side.' A cry came from the top of the mainmast.

The Quartermaster and Captain looked out to the port side. As the Captain looked with his telescope, the Quartermaster asked, taking out his own, 'Can you see it, Captain?'

'Looks like a clipper. I'm not sure. Now, a clipper is one large mast, with a square staysail and a forward course jib?'

'No, Captain. A clipper has three masts and is square rigged.'

'What am I thinking of then?' The Captain searched his brain, trying to remember what class of ship looked like what he could see.

'Probably a cutter, Captain,' The Quartermaster replied helpfully.

'Cutter, yes.'

The Quartermaster looked at the unknown vessel through his telescope.

'But it looks more like a sloop to me.'

'Sloop. You sure?'

'Fairly, I mean.' The Quartermaster hesitated before adding, 'It is a few miles away, it's true, Captain, but a cutter is a small single-mast boat, fore-and-aft rigged with two or more headsails, usually carried on a very long bowsprit, whereas a sloop is agile, with a shallow draft, rigged with a large mainsail, attached to a spar and sports both additional square and lateen-rigged sails, just like that one.' He nodded to the boat on the horizon. 'Has a large mainsail across its mast. Oh, and a sloop is very fast, can do 12 knots.'

'So it's most likely to be a sloop,' the Captain summed up as he gazed at the unknown boat a little more through his telescope.

'I'd say so, Captain. They're catching us pretty fast.'

'Probably empty,' the Captain shrugged, 'probably just sold all their cargo in Kingston and are now heading on to Miami or Charlestown I suspect.'

'Empty, Captain?' the Quartermaster queried.

'Aye, empty.' He folded his telescope away. 'How else would they be able to travel at such a speed?'

'But, sir, it's not usual for a merchant ship to sail without some cargo. I mean, we never do, Captain.'

'Ah but yes,' the Captain replied. 'They probably work for the Osborn, Haig, Cameron and Johnson trading company. They're well known for all their empty promises.'

'But didn't they go bust, sir, taking all their industry down with them, leaving everything in ruin and now making their money talking about how to run a successful trading company amongst the great and the good in Boston, Washington, Richmond, Paris and Torquay?'

Before the Captain could reply, from above the mainsail a cry echoed, 'Sail, starboard side.'

The Captain and the Quartermaster headed over to the starboard side of the deck and through their telescopes they looked out towards the new sail on the horizon.

'What's that? A brigantine?'

'Brig, Captain.' The Quartermaster replied. 'We're a brigantine.'

'You sure, Quartermaster?' the Captain asked wearily.

'A brig is a vessel with two square-rigged masts. The aft mast carries a small gaff-rigged fore-and-aft sail,' The Quartermaster began. 'A brigantine has no lateen sails, is square-rigged on the foremast and has a gaff-rigged mainsail with square rig above. Their main mast is the aft one and our ship is smaller than that.' He pointed over to the brig heading their way.

'How can you tell. It's far away. They all look small far away!'

'But it's clearly bigger than a sloop, Captain, much bigger, and wider.'

The Captain looked through his telescope.

'They're unfurling a flag.' Then his face turned ashen with shock. 'A black flag. It's a man sharing a jug or something with a skeleton.'

'Pirate flag, ho,' a voice cried from the crow's nest.

'We know. We can see it.' The Captain shouted back.

'Port side, Captain,' came the lookout's reply.

Quickly the Captain and the Quartermaster rushed over to the port side.

'Another black flag, this time a skull's head over two crossed swords.'

'Looks like we're going to be boarded, Captain, by two pirate ships!'

'What action should we take?' the Captain asked. 'Have we enough guns?'

'Two ships, sir. They'll slaughter us!'

The Captain moved to the front of the quarterdeck. He could see Cay Sal still ahead of him.

'Helm, steer for that headland. Maybe once we pass it,

we'll have the wind to outrun them.'

The Quartermaster sighed as the Helm turned the wheel when suddenly the sails began to ripple and hang loose as The Jill slowed.

A few minutes later, the two pirate ships came along either side of The Jill.

2

The Captain rushed to the rail, looking down to the main deck as the grappling irons clattered and bit into the side of the bulwarks.

'Prepare to repel boarders!' the Captain cried.

'Which?' his Quartermaster asked.

'Name-calling's not very helpful at the moment.'

'I mean, Captain, we've 75 men, and there could be up to a hundred and forty on each pirate ship.'

'Bit of a bummer really, isn't it?' The Captain sighed disheartened.

The Quartermaster nodded his agreement, as the sound of a gunshot echoed and then some pirates from both ships swung across, swarming over The Jill's decks.

The Captain turned white with fear as he saw, coming from the bigger ship, named The Fortune, the pirate rabble was led, by a dark-skinned, rough-looking man in an old Royal Navy coat, his flintlock drawn and a cutlass in his mouth which he took hold off as he let the rope fall from his grasp. From the other side, two pirates caught the Captain's eye, a suave-looking man with a kindly face wearing calico trousers, brandishing two flintlocks, and, standing next to him, a slim woman dressed like a man, with long jet-black hair and a burning fire in her eyes, gun and sword to hand. She scared him the most.

'Surrender or die!' the dark-skinned rogue shouted, firing across the bow of The Jill and hitting a red-coated pirate from the smaller vessel, who dropped his own flintlock and cried out in pain as he held his arm.

'They just shot Fenwick.' The female pirate cried to the one in the calico trousers.

'No, we didn't,' the Captain cried, holding up his hands. Fearing the worst, he added, 'We surrender.'

'It's alright. It's only a flesh wound,' the pirate in the red coat cried back.

'I would never shoot anyone!' the Captain continued, as the pirate in the calico trousers and the dark-skinned rogue both turned to him. 'I hate the sight of blood, especially mine.'

The dark-skinned rogue smirked apologetically and shrugged. As he held his gun up, he called over to the other pirates.

'Sorry. That was my fault.'

The pirate in the calico trousers and the woman pirate stepped forwards to meet him. A broad smile came across their faces as they recognised each other.

'Black Bart. What are you doing here?' the pirate in the calico trousers cried.

Bartholomew Roberts, also known as Black Bart, was a successful pirate, known for his big ships, fancy dress sense, and sinking ships that resisted his crew's attempts to pillage them.

'Calico Jack, Quartermaster Bonny, what a pleasant surprise!' Bart replied.

Calico Jack Rackham, one-time Quartermaster to Charles Vane and lover to Anne Bonny, who became his Quartermaster when they took The Neptune from Vane's squadron and set up in business for themselves. 'I didn't know you were waiting off Cay Sal,' Bart added.

'We've been here three days waiting for this ship,' Calico Jack replied.

'I admire your dedication, Jack. I admire it. I do, I really do.'

'We going to be long, Captain, only it's nearly two?' A small portly guy with a short black beard and a cutlass in his hand asked Black Bart as he came up to stand next to him. Black Bart waved him down a moment as Jack replied.

'The thing is, Bart, we've not had a sniff for three days. Surely this prize should be ours. I mean. We did get here first.'

'Yes, Jack, but we've got 26 cannon. You've only got six.' Black Bart grinned, scratching his cheek with the muzzle of his gun.

'We've got four swivel guns as well,' Jack replied defensively, his pride for his little sloop a little dented by Black Bart's remark.

Bart held his hands up. 'Pardon me. Thing is, Jack, there's probably enough cargo for us both.'

'But only half as much,' Anne replied, her thick Irish accent cutting through like a hot knife through butter, 'I mean, you know the rules, Bart, we can't take it all or we'd put the merchants out of business and then we'd have no ships to rob.'

'Captain. The time,' the portly pirate reminded Black Bart.

'Alright, Coates.' Black Bart sighed. 'In a minute.' Then he turned back to Jack. 'Think we need to parley.'

'Guys, if it's any help, we don't mind who robs us. Only we'd like to be on our way as soon as possible,' the Captain of The Jill interrupted.

'We sure would,' added his Quartermaster. 'We've both got hot dates in Miami, so if you could.'

'Yeah, you wish!' Anne rounded on them coldly as Bart sighed, turning to the Captain.

'Alright, alright, keep your hair on. Me and Jack have got a couple of details to sort out, so button it.'

The Captain and the Quartermaster nodded.

'Your ship or mine?' Bart asked, turning back to Jack once more.

'Well, as you've got a cabin on the Fortune all to yourself, shall we use yours?' Jack asked.

3

Black Bart sat behind his desk with Jack and Anne sitting opposite. On the desk between them there was a bottle of wine. They had a glass each and were smoking big fat Cuban cigars.

'So, Jack, you want to divvy up the spoils of this prize?' Bart began, blowing a ring of smoke into the air.

'It's only fair, Bart. I mean, we were here first.'

There was a knock at the door and Coates entered carrying The Jill's manifest, which he handed to Black Bart.

'The men, sir,' he reminded his captain, nodding to the deck above.

'I'll be with you in couple of minutes,' Bart assured him as he opened the manifest and held it up slightly so that the light from the wall of small square windows behind him could illuminate the pages.

'Very good, Captain.' Coates grinned and left.

'Yes.' Bart took his cigar and placed it down on the desk as he took a sip of wine before continuing. 'Looking at this, I think there's enough rum and sugar to split it. Only....' he grinned.... 'my men have found the medicine chest and that's mine.' He picked up his cigar again and took a deep, satisfying puff.

'But the chest's worth at least £300!' Jack exclaimed. 'That's 24,000 pieces of eight back in New Providence!'

Bart smiled and blew a smoke ring high into the air.

'Surely we can share that too,' Jack pleaded.

'Not with my 26 guns we don't,' Bart replied with a broad grin.

'Now look here, you lazy, good-for-nothing, low-life product of a sow's arse.' Anne slammed the desk with her fist as she continued. 'We have as much right to a share of that medicine chest as any of your toerags on your rotting heap of junk.'

'I can offer you a single share each as if you were sailors on my ship,' Bart replied as he began to work out how many shares that would be. 'What, there's what on The Neptune, twelve of you? Twelve single shares, I can't say fairer that that.'

'But there's nigh on one hundred and forty on the Fortune!' she cried.

'Darling.' Jack held her gently by the arm. 'Not so angry, my love. We're negotiating.'

'With his dick up your arse. I don't call that a negotiation,' she huffed.

'Take it or leave it, or let's duke it out.' Bart shrugged. 'Remember, I've got 26 to your six. Even if you count your swivel guns, I still have the advantage.'

Jack turned to Anne who gave him a demon of a look, so that he felt a pang in his soul as if she was already roasting it over a fire with a bag full of chestnuts.

'But Bart.' He turned back to Black Bart. 'If my boys find out we let a medicine chest slip through our fingers, the guys, well, you know, they might want to take a vote.'

'Not my problem.' He blew another smoke ring as he sat back in his chair, his smile growing ever wider.

'But surely, there's something you can give me?' Jack pleaded. 'Maybe we could have a couple of extra barrels of sugar?'

Bart reflected on that suggestion for a moment before he replied.

'Problem is Jack, me old fellow, if my lads see us take less sugar than you, then they're likely to want a vote too. You're alright. You've got Anne there on your side. Me! If they don't lynch me, they'll dump me on some empty island, Jack. See it from my point of view. I can't be seen to be doing you any favours without the lads thinking I've gone all soft.'

'So you're going to bash us with your droopy dick whilst we have a vote on our hands!' Anne snapped back.

Just then there was a knock on the door as Coates entered.

'Captain. It's time,' he reminded him.

'I'll be right up.'

Coates left as they finished their drinks and as they all stood, Bart began.

'Look. Stay for a while, Jack.' He came around the desk and put his arm on Jack's shoulder. 'Let's let the guys unload and I think I might have something for you, which I think will solve both our problems.'

'Really, Bart. You mean that?'

They headed out as Bart replied, 'Jack, my lad, trust me.'

Anne just rolled her eyes as she followed them men out, fearing the worse.

4

They joined Coates up by the rail of the quarterdeck, looking down on the whole of the Fortune's crew gathered on the main deck below, and as Coates blew into a pitch pipe, the whole crew began to sing one of Bart's favourite songs that reminded him of his homeland, Rhyfelgyrch Gwŷr Harlech as one man.

Black Bart turned to Anne and Jack.

'Rules of my ship. We have a chorus at two and another before bed. Keeps the men's spirits up.'

'Thing is, Bart,' Jack replied, 'I need more than you're offering if I'm going to keep my men's spirits up.'

'Just calm down. Like I told you, I have something that should keep your crew happy.' He put his arm around Jack and led him and Anne to the rear of the boat. 'What if I told you, that on this ship's manifest there's a lucrative pickup of cotton cloth to be had and that, because my hull's full and I need to get back to Nassau, I'm giving you the manifest and I'm giving you the prize to pick it up and bring it back to Nassau.'

'They were going to pick up some cotton cloth?' Jack sighed. 'Have to be a lot of it to make up £300.'

'Who cares, stupid, that's what you tell your men before you set sail.' Bart sighed. 'That way, they can't protest once they know what you're really getting, 'cos if you tell them beforehand, they might not want to go get it.'

'So what will we actually be getting?' Anne asked suspiciously.

'Well, to be honest with you, if we hadn't taken this prize, we were on our way to Boston.'

'Why?' she asked.

'To pick up gunpowder.' He smiled.

'You mean, you were running gunpowder to New Providence.'

'How else do you think we get enough powder to see off the Royal Navy. It doesn't grow on trees you know.'

'No?' continued Anne. 'But you do make it with charcoal which is made from trees!'

'Well?' Anne and Jack looked at each other as if they were thinking about that idea as Bart continued. 'It's all paid for. My contact in Port Royal fixed it for me. Well, I say my contact. Really he's one of Hornigold's contacts, but it's all bought and paid for. All you've got to do is head up to Boston, ask for Jean-Luc at the Red Lion and bring back sixty barrels of the best powder this side of the Atlantic. Proper British stuff, milled at Faversham.'

'So only the best then.' Anne was impressed.

'Sixty barrels. That will fill our hold.' Jack agreed.

'And worth three hundred after costs, transportation fees and so forth in New Providence. Same as the medicine chest and all you got to do is sail there and bring it back to me. I'll finish the deal and square it all up with you. I mean, what is it? An extra week at sea?' Black Bart asked as he waited for Jack to answer.

Jack thought for a moment, then turning to Anne, he asked, 'What do you think Anne?'

'You got a letter of introduction for us?' she asked Bart.

'Why of course,' he replied taking a letter out of his coat's inner pocket and handing it to her. She opened and read it.

'It all seems in order.' She turned to Jack. 'We'll take it.'

'Good.' Bart slapped Jack affectionately on the back. 'I knew you'd see sense. Look, do you want to stay for the next couple of songs?'

'No.' Jack shook his head. 'I think we should check on how things are loading and cut along as soon as we can.'

'Fine. Happy sailing and I'll see you back in Nassau, Jack.'

'See you back there, Bart.'

'Anne.' Bart nodded to her.

'Bart.' She responded with a small nod back to him.

Jack and Anne crossed over the gangplanks to the merchant ship and then over to The Neptune.

5

It wasn't long before The Neptune was back, all alone, at sea, with Davis at the helm. Jack was on the quarterdeck with his trusty old navigator Bourn, who had a map spread out over a barrel they kept tied by the rail overlooking the main deck. He was checking the compass before looking back at the map and ensuring he had the map orientated in the right direction.

Bourn looked over the main deck and called out, 'What's our speed?'

Howell, who was holding a line over the side, was letting the knotted rope slowly drift through his fingers. Standing beside him was young Earl, keeping an eye on his watch.

'Time,' Earl cried, then snapped his watch-lid shut.

'Six knots,' Howell shouted back to Bourn and, then started to pull the rope back up into a coil.

Bourn looked at the map as Jack peered over it with him.

'We're making good time, Captain. At this rate we'll be in Boston by noon tomorrow.'

'Good. Keep us on a steady course, Mr Davis.'

'Aye, Captain,' Davis called back, holding the wheel tightly.

*

Sure enough, by two the next day, they were in Boston. Leaving the rest of the crew to tidy they ship and make ready for their journey back, Jack, with Anne, Fenwick and Dobbins, left the harbour and went off into the streets of Boston in search of The Red Lion Inn.

They soon found it and, as they sat round a table drinking a well-deserved ale from their pewter tankards, Jean-Luc arrived.

He was a weasel-faced man with a slim moustache and had a constant whiff of onions and garlic about him. As he stood in the doorway, looking at all the fine British merchants and the red-coated soldiers, he noticed Jack and his crew, more withdrawn, trying hard to blend in and not be seen. He knew these just had to be his contacts and so crossed over to them.

Speaking from behind his hand, he asked Jack. 'You Black Bart?' in his thick French accent.

'Sort of,' Jack replied as Jean-Luc sat between him and Anne, his smell making them both pinch their noses.

'What do you mean? Sort of?'

'Black Bart sent us. Anne, the letter.'

She took it from her coat pocket. 'Here.' And thrust it into Jean-Luc's hand. Quickly he read it.

'Everything seem to be in order.' He folded it closed again and handed it back to her. 'You are here for the Black Bart cargo, no?'

'Well, yes!' Jack replied.

'Then you will have to come with me, on a journey up the back passage.'

'Look, we just want the cargo,' Jack replied, a little startled.

'Yes, yes, this is the cargo,' Jean-Luc assured him. 'It up the hill, in the wilderness. I keep it up my back passage and you can take it there, no.'

Jack turned to Anne. She shrugged.

'Either way, I'm game.'

'Okay.' Jack turned his attention back to Jean-Luc. 'How far are these hills?'

'In the direction in the way the crow fly, it is two mile.'

'And by road?'

'Fourteen.'

'Then we're going to have to hire a cart and horses.' Jack sighed and turned to his crewmen. 'Dobbins, you and Fenwick arrange that. We'll get the rest of the crew and meet back here. That alright, Jen?

'Jean-Luc.' he corrected Jack, who shrugged.

'Whatever!'

The French could be really touchy at times.

6

The forest of trees seemed as tall as the mountains and with their stretched-out canopy of needle-like leaves, they crowded out the sky, so that little sunlight shone through, making it dark and dank. Fenwick and Jean-Luc's fur-trapper friend led the way. Each of them was armed with a flintlock, musket and sword and Jack, Jean-Luc, Anne, Davies, Bourn, Dobbins, Earl, Corner, Howell, Harwood and Carty, followed in two lines. Their horses walked with their heads down, grabbing a quick bite of any fern leaves that brushed by their nose.

'So where did you get all this cargo, Jean-Luc?' Anne asked, fidgeting slightly in her saddle. It had been a long time since she'd left Charlestown, which was the last time she had ridden a horse.

'It sort of fell off a cart on its way to Fort William Henry.' Jean-Luc replied.

Dobbins wiped the back of his neck with an old piece of cloth. The muggy air was making him sweat and he was being bitten alive by all the midges.

'Is it much further, Captain?' he called. Jack turned to Jean-Luc.

'No,' Jean-Luc replied, 'over the next rise.'

Dobbins turned to Davis, who was riding at his side.

'Typical.' He threw his head back in disgust. 'We're sailors, not bloody cavalry. If I had wanted to sign up to ride a horse, I'd have joined the army!'

'At least they're easier to steer,' Davis replied helpfully.

'What do you mean? I keep pulling the reins and nothing happens.'

'I know, but you don't need to steer them. They know where they're going.'

Dobbins sighed.

*

Another hour passed before they reached the rocky mountain road. They slowly climbed the steep slope, riding along the ridge. It was another hour before they reached the plateau, about halfway up, where the mountain divided itself into two peaks. At the base of one peak, there was a cave.

There was a lot of old brush and branches that had been scattered around the opening of the cave. A large wooden door, that had been built across it, had been ripped off its iron hinges, and was hanging by just one nail, at an angle, half upright and wide open, showing the dark black tunnel behind.

The fur trapper held up his hand and they brought their horses to a stop. Staring in disbelief at the sight before him, Jean-Luc cried. 'Mon dieu! I have been robbed.'

Fenwick, Anne, Jean-Luc, the fur trapper, Jack and

Dobbins all quickly got off their horses and went over to the wreckage of Jean-Luc's hideaway.

There was total confusion as the fur trapper and Jean-Luc quickly rushed into the cave while the others stood just outside and waited. Then as Jean-Luc and the man returned, shaking their heads, Jean-Luc turned to the others.

'It looks like we have been robbed by Indians.'

'Indians? Here?' Jack cried. He and his crew unslung their muskets, their eyes nervously scanning the surrounding trees and rocks.

'Yes.' Jean-Luc shrugged. 'This is Indian country.'

'What would Indians want with gunpowder?' Anne asked. 'They don't have any cannon, do they?'

'No,' Jean-Luc replied with a shake of his head as he continued, 'but they take not just gunpowder, but also my fur, my wine, my sugar, my cloth. They have taken the lot!' He looked at Jack. 'We may be in luck, as if they were taken by my friends, then they will give you back the gunpowder.'

'And if not?' Jack asked.

'Then you may have to fight to get it back.'

'Fair enough,' Jack agreed.

'And just who are your friends?' Anne asked.

'Why, the Mohican, of course,' Jean-Luc continued. 'If they have taken my store, then they will give you back your gunpowder, that I promise. I just hope they are not the Pawnee, as they do not like me very much.'

'And how will we know which ones are these Mohicans?' she asked.

'They have long hair down the middle of the head, but shave both sides and wear two feathers in their hair.'

'And the Pawnee?'

'They too have long hair down the middle of the head, but shave both sides and wear two feathers in their hair.'

They all looked at Jean-Luc bemused.

'Then how do we know who to parley with and who to fight?' Dobbins asked with a heavy sigh.

'The Pawnee wear their feathers on one side only. The Mohican one feather on each side,' Jean-Luc replied helpfully.

'Then why didn't you say that in the first place, you flat-faced arse of a frog!' Anne snapped and gritted her teeth, resisting the urge to put her cutlass through his chest.

'We will have to cross the river. I know my friends camp near there.'

Jack turned to Anne as she looked to him for advice and just shrugged.

7

They backtracked through the woods for half an hour before they headed west and after another half hour, they had reached a clearing in the woods that opened out onto a bend of a wide, fast-flowing river. The trapper signalled them to stop and they all started to dismount.

'Why are we getting off the horses here?' Jack asked, coming over to stand by Jean-Luc.

'The river is too deep,' he told him. 'We will have to find a new way to cross.'

As Jack, Jean-Luc, the fur trapper, Anne and Dobbins came closer to the water's edge, there was a sudden whoosh, and the trapper, holding his chest from which an arrow was sticking out, cried out in pain and staggered back a pace before falling to the ground dead.

'Indians!' Jean-Luc screamed.

'Where?' Jack cried looking all around him as there

was another whoosh and an arrow struck the tree, right between Jack and Anne. As they looked at the arrow, the crew readied their muskets.

'Put your guns away. These are my friends.' Jean-Luc replied as he pointed to the feathers on the arrow.

Another whoosh and Fenwick fell to the floor with an arrow in the back of his shoulder.

'Anyone would think we were at an Irish wedding with this many guys hitting the deck!' Anne sighed.

'Fenwick, you alright?' Jack called.

'I'm fine, Captain,' he replied, getting back to his feet. 'It's only a flesh wound.'

Suddenly they were surrounded by Pawnee Indians as instinctively the pirates dropped their weapons and along with Jean-Luc held up their hands to surrender.

'Well,' Jean-Luc sighed. 'Anybody can make a mistake!'

*

They were tied together in one long line and led along the river bank until, as the sun began to set behind the mountains, they reached the Indian encampment.

Fenwick, who still had the arrow sticking out the back of his shoulder, Jack, Anne, Jean-Luc, Davies, Bourn, Dobbins, Earl, Corner, Howell, Harwood, and Carty were all tied to a long pole supported on two stakes. All but Anne were stripped down to the waist as around a large fire that blazed before them, the Indian warriors danced and chanted, waving their tomahawks and spears as they kicked up the dust, whilst the young boys and the rest of the tribe watched on and feasted in celebration.

'I had always believed I would die at sea,' Dobbins sighed ruefully.

'The Pawnee have a fierce reputation,' Jean-Luc began. 'They are great warrior people. Even the women are strong warriors.'

'So, what now?' Dobbins asked. 'Are they just going to kill us?'

'Oh, no, they will torture us first,' Jean-Luc replied.

'Charming!'

'It is not too bad. Here there are beasts in the forest who can eat a man in one bite!'

'You mean they would eat me whole?' Anne asked a little nervously.

'Why not. It's your best feature.' Jack replied.

'Can't we reason with their chief, Captain?' Dobbins asked.

'No use.' Jean-Luc shrugged. 'They are a society ruled by women.'

'So we're sunk then!' Jack agreed.

The warrior leader and two other warriors, emerged from a tepee on the far side of the fire with a young woman. She had a noble bearing and the three men walked a pace behind her, as they made their way towards their prisoners.

Then as they stood just a few yards away from them, the young woman whispered into the warrior leader's ear. He listened, turned to her and said something which none of the crew could hear.

'Suppose she's deciding which one of us to torture first!' Dobbins cried.

'I hope it's not with fire,' Bourn replied. 'Only it's a bit too hot to be burnt to death.'

'Well, excuse me.' Dobbins sighed as he rolled his eyes. 'Next time we get captured by the Pawnee, I'll put a request in for us to be tortured with ice for you, shall I, Bourn?'

The warrior leader led the young woman over to stand before Jack, Anne and Jean-Luc.

'I am Silver Leaf,' she began calmly with an air of absolute authority. 'I am the chief of this tribe until my mother comes back from a hunting trip in Oregon. Who are you and why are you on Pawnee land?'

'Nice to meet you, Silver Leaf.' Jack smiled warmly. 'My name's, Jack, Jack Rackham. I'm captain of The Neptune and this is my crew. Well, except for Jean-Luc there.' He nodded towards Jean-Luc. 'He's the one we've come to see, you see. He's sold us some gunpowder, which we're trading to sell for other goods back on New Providence Island.'

Silver Leaf held up a hand to stop him talking.

'Why is that one still wearing his shirt?' she asked looking at Anne.

'That's not a man,' the warrior leader replied.

'That's my Quartermaster, Anne Bonny, Miss Silver Leaf,' Jack added helpfully.

Silver Leaf stood back a pace and looked Anne up and down. She turned to the warrior leader with a quizzical look on her face. The warrior nodded once and then Silver Leaf stepped forward and groped Anne's breasts.

'You really are a woman,' Silver Leaf commented as if she was impressed.

'So, what you going to do about it, you feather-wearing, tree-hugging freak?' Anne snapped back at her. 'If I wasn't tied to this pole, I'd rip your bloody head off and piss down your throat.'

Silver Leaf smiled, impressed by Anne's outburst, as she folded her arms and looked Anne up and down once more.

'Bring her to my tepee.'

'Yes, chief.' the warrior leader agreed.

Silver Leaf turned and walked away to her tepee, as the other two Indians with the warrior leader cut Anne down. Holding her arms as she tried to wriggle and kick free, they followed the warrior leader to Silver Leaf's tepee.

8

The night wore on and, as the Indians danced around the large fire, groans and cries echoed from Silver Leaf's tepee while Jack and his fellow captives helplessly just hung around awaiting their fate.

'Six hours,' Dobbins moaned. 'What cruel and unnatural tortures are they subjecting poor Anne to?'

'I don't know,' Bourn replied, 'but I sure hope our fates are not so drawn out.'

The flap to the tepee opened and Anne, her trousers undone, her shirt all buttoned up wrong and un-tucked, stepped out, followed moments later by Silver Leaf, her feathers crumpled and her dress off at one shoulder, both looking like they'd just got dressed in a hurry. The two of them had huge smiles on their faces and looked at peace.

Slowly, hand-in-hand they made their way around the fire. As Silver Leaf and Anne reached the others, the

Indians around the fire stopped dancing and the warrior leader crossed over to them both.

'I have had a long....' Silver Leaf thought carefully for a moment, '..... discussion with my new friend Anne, and she has opened my eyes to new ideas as I have opened hers likewise. I hereby, as a favour to my new friend, grant you all safe passage back to Boston and you may take your gun....' Silver Leaf let out a huge exhausted yawn, before she continued, '....powder with you.'

The other Indians started to cut their prisoners down.

*

By first light the next day, they were at sea again, and it wasn't long before they had reached New Providence and the safety of Nassau Harbour.

*

At the inn, Black Bart was sitting with two of his crew at a table drinking ale when Jack, Anne and Dobbins entered and came over to them.

'Jack, saw you were back, and you brought the gunpowder. You didn't have any trouble, did you?' Bart asked raising his tankard to him as they reached his table.

'Not a problem, Bart.'

The barmaid brought over three ales and passed them around Jack and his crew.

'Didn't have any trouble with those Indians?' Bart asked.

'Not really,' Jack replied, adding, 'Anne gave their chief a right tongue lashing, didn't you, love?' Anne choked on her beer as Jack continued. 'The chief took her into her tent thingy and they bashed away for hours. Didn't you, love?'

'I certainly saw her point, if that's what you mean.' Anne smiled.

'Well, good for you, Jack.' Bart turned to the landlord behind his counter. 'Landlord, drinks all round on me.'

'Thanks, Bart.' Jack patted Black Bart on the shoulder.

'That's fine, Jack.' The barmaid returned with six jugs of ale and passed them around the table. 'You deserve it. I'll have my bank transfer the funds this afternoon.'

9

There was a slight breeze coming off the Kingston Harbour as the stagecoach arrived outside the elegant three-floor, red-brick governor's residence.

Three steps flanked by an ornamental balustrade led down from the front door. A footman descended and crossed over to open the coach doors. He lowered the step and out climbed Woodes Rodgers, a tall elegant man, though a bit chubby of face, wearing a long, brown, curly wig, followed by his fat, frumpy wife.

'Well, sweetheart,' Woodes began as he helped her disembark. 'Here it is, our new residence for the next ten years.'

She looked around and sighed disheartened. She cried, 'What a dump!'

'Oh, precious, I'm sure it's lovely inside.' He stood back so she could look up at the house in its full splendour.

'When I agreed to marry you and you took the role of governor, I thought we were going to be sent to some cushy little number, not chasing smugglers. Somewhere civilised like Boston, or Charlestown. Not Kingston.'

'But darling,' he protested. 'This is an important part of the British Empire in the Caribbean.' She rolled her eyes and grunted as he continued. 'But precious, to get a placement like Boston takes a lot of bribes and backhanders. We don't have enough money to pay the normal Tory backhander rate of fifty thousand pounds, never mind the bribes for the colonists! You know, dearest, all my business interests have failed. If I hadn't taken this job, which no one wants, we'd be in the workhouse and you don't want that, do you, my love of my life?'

Mrs Rodgers pushed past him and the footman and stormed off into the house.

'If you would see to our luggage,' he politely asked the footman as he readjusted his wig.

'Sir.' The footman bowed and then started to arrange the unloading of the coach as Woodes reluctantly followed his wife into the house.

*

His office faced onto the well-kept gardens that ran down to, and seemed to disappear into, the forests at the end of the property.

His desk faced into the room so he had his back to the tall window and the light behind him made it easy to see everything on it in the dark, oak-panelled room.

He looked around, admiring his new upturn in fortune. Then, after a short while, he opened a drawer in which there was a bit of black cloth. He smiled warmly to himself as he took it out and, holding it fondly, looked at it, letting his mind drift off to much happier times.

10

It was two years before that, a pirate ship, The Duke, which was a ketch, a two-masted vessel, square-rigged, with a large sail on the mainmast and with a smaller mizzen, closed on the twin-masted lugger.

Standing proudly on The Duke's quarterdeck, dressed in his rough pirate clothes, with a huge grin on his face, was Woodes, looking through his telescope as they closed on the lugger.

'Fire two shots across her bows!' he cried. Pike, his Quartermaster, a tall lanky lad with thin, straw-like blond hair, replied, 'Aye, Captain,' and turned to face the main deck.

He gave the order. 'Fire two shots across her bows.'

Moments later, The Duke fired two shots, the cannonballs splashing harmlessly into the sea a few yards ahead of their quarry.

Woodes put his telescope away as they closed steadily on the lugger.

'Prepare to board!' he cried as he checked his flintlock and cutlass. Then with Quartermaster Pike, he headed down to the main deck.

*

The two ships touched and The Duke's crew threw their grappling hooks. As they landed on the lugger, Captain Howard, a pompous little man, turned to Master Miles, his Quartermaster and ex-slave, and shouted, 'Cut the ropes.'

'It's too late!' Miles cried as the ships bumped together for the second time.

Gangplanks suddenly rattled as they were allowed to fall to bridge between the two ships. Other pirates swung across on ropes, followed a couple of moments later by Woodes and Pike.

As Miles led his half-dozen crew to the side of the ship, their swords drawn, ready to repel the pirates, he was kicked in the face by Woodes still swinging on his rope, falling backwards into two of his men and they all collapsed into a heap on the deck.

Howard, holding his sword, ran over to the helm as the pirates began to swarm across his ship and he watched in horror as his crew, threw down their weapons and surrendered, putting their hands up and kneeling down. Woodes looked around and, seeing where Howard stood, called a couple of others with him as he rushed for the lugger's helm.

'Surrender now or I'll kill the lot of you. I'll sink you and let you all drown!' Woodes cried, rushing at Howard as the captain pushed his helmsman forward to keep him between the pirates and himself.

'Fight them, you dogs,' Howard encouraged his men, waving his sword above his head. 'Think of the cargo!'

Woodes rushed them and the Helm dropped to his knees as Howard swung at Woodes.

With a swift flick of the wrist, he parried him away then thumped him square in the face with the cutlass's hand guard.

Howard sank to the floor holding his nose.

'You've broken my nose!' he cried.

'He normally does.' Pike shrugged coming to Woodes' side.

Woodes walked away, putting his cutlass back in his belt and turned to his men. They had taken the lugger swiftly and none of them had been hurt. With a joyful cry, he called to them, 'Men, load the cargo,' and was greeted with a huge cheer.

*

The weapons were picked up, the lugger's crew were all taken to the farthest side of the ship with a couple of men standing guard over them, and the rest of the pirate crew quickly loaded some of the barrels of rum, sacks of corn and sugar into The Duke's hold.

When they were done, the merchant crew watched as the pirates swung back across, leaving only Pike and Woodes still on their ship.

'I'll have the Royal Navy after you for this,' Howard promised them sullenly. 'This, this is the sixth time you've robbed us.'

'I suggest you go a different route.' Pike sighed and then swung across to The Duke.

'I'll tell the governor!' Howard cried.

'Like that corrupt backslider's going to do anything.' Woodes laughed then swung back too.

*

Soon they had disentangled the ships, and within a

couple of days they were back in New Providence and safe in Nassau Harbour.

11

There were a lot of pirates at the inn.

For the most part it was standing room only as every table was taken and there was a mad scrambling horde clamouring for service at the counter.

At one table was Charles Vane, a bearded, rough-looking man with a round face and hard, staring eyes, and at another, the opposite side of the Inn, sat Calico Jack with Anne Bonny and their boatswain James Dobbins.

There was a roaring noise as lots of drinking, lots of swearing and lots of boasting filled the air when Woodes and Pike, entered.

'Another successful trip, Pike.' He put his arm around Pike's shoulders.

'I agree, Captain.'

'I think we deserve a drink, don't you?'

'Right you are, Captain.' Pike nodded.

They headed towards the bar, acknowledging Vane and then Calico Jack and Anne as they passed.

They fought their way through and waited a short while for the landlord to come over to them.

As the landlord leant on the counter looking at them both, Woodes held up two fingers and cried, 'Two ales, landlord.'

'Right you are, Captain Rodgers.' The landlord held aloft two fingers and moved to a barrel behind him to fill two tankards with ale.

'Busy today,' Woodes commented as the landlord peered back at him over his shoulder.

'Well, Friday is the BAPTAs, Captain Rodgers.'

'The what?'

'BAPTAs, sir.' Pike replied. 'Bahamas Annual Pirate Testimonial Awards, sir.'

The landlord placed the first tankard on the table as he continued, 'It's the festival we have once every year to honour New Providence's best pirates.'

'How do you get nominated?' Woodes asked interestedly.

'Being based in New Providence, Captain.' The landlord finished filling the second tankard and gave it to Pike as Woodes paid with two coins.

'And it's this Friday?' he asked as the landlord took the coins.

'That's right, sir. All the pirates will be here by Friday. Well, all that's based here, that is.'

Woodes and Pike raised their drinks.

'To the BAPTAs!' Woodes toasted as they struck their tankards together.

12

That night, as the torch fires burned in their coconut shells aligned along either side of the long blue carpet stretching from the inn to the street behind, a large crowd stood in the street.

As the pirates arrived, the crowd waved, cheered and chanted their names while the press, standing close to the carpet, tried to attract their attention to get an exclusive interview.

Black Bart's coach pulled up and he stepped out, waving to the crowd, and made his way along the carpet to the inn door, where he turned back to them and waved some more. Just then another coach pulled up as Black Bart's moved away, and out of it stepped, the suave and yet dangerously cruel-looking Captain Ed Lowe.

The local reporter, Mel Perkins, dressed in her off-the-shoulder smock and with her afro combed back into a bun, waved to Captain Lowe.

'Captain Lowe.' He saw her and sauntered over, adjusting the cuffs of his coat as he approached. 'Captain Lowe,' she asked, taking out her chalk and slate, 'a quick word for the Bahamas and Bridgetown Chronicle.'

'Sure.' He smiled with a gritty charm that almost melted her heart. 'Anything for the BBC.'

Next to Mel, her assistant took out a pad and charcoal and started to draw a portrait of Captain Lowe.

'Captain Lowe, can I ask you, are you looking forward to the night?'

He thought for a moment.

'Yes, I am, Mel.' He shot her a killer smile and continued, 'It's been a good year this year. There's a lot of new crews out there. Charles Vane's had a lot of success. I think it's going to be a really interesting event.'

'And as our readers would like to know, whose coat are you wearing this year?'

'Why....' He looked at it and opened it slightly so she could see its sumptuous silk lining. '....Samson's of Port Royal.'

He then started to make his way along the line, heading for the door, just as another coach arrived.

'Thanks, Captain Lowe' Mel cried, her attention turning to the new coach. 'Oh, look, I've just seen Captain Rodgers arrive.'

Woodes made his way up the carpet.

'Captain Rodgers, Captain Rodgers!' Mel called, waving to him and, as he came over to her, she asked, 'A quick word for the Bahamas and Bridgetown Chronicle?'

'Sure.'

Her assistant found a new page in his pad and started to draw Woodes.

'Captain Rodgers, can I ask you, are you looking forward to the night?'

He smiled and held his hands up as if to deflect any praise.

'Yes, I am, thank you, Mel. It's been a good year this year. There's a lot of new crews out there. I think it's going to be a really interesting event. I might even have a good chance of winning the best newcomer award.'

'It's a close-fought category this year, you know. Captain Rackham, who used to sail under Charles Vane, is in that category too and he has experience even if this is his first awards season as a captain.'

'Like I said,' Woodes smiled, 'should be interesting. But may I just say, Mel, may the best man,' he pointed to himself, 'win, if you know what I mean. Eh? Eh?'

'Well, good luck,' she replied, adding, 'Oh, and one last question, as our readers would like to know, whose coat are you wearing this year?'

'Why, Jenkins of Bridgetown, Jamaica.' Then, with that, he made his way along the carpet as another coach arrived.

*

There was a stage set up next to the bar, as all the tables were filled with pirates, each facing towards the stage with their quartermasters and key crew on their tables with them. It seemed every pirate of note was there. Along with Black Bart, Ed Lowe, Woodes Rodgers, Charles Vane, Jack Rackham with Anne Bonny and Dobbins, there was Edward Teach with his mad staring eyes, who was also known as Blackbeard, because of his bushy black beard, the tall and elegant 'Black Sam' Samuel Bellamy, who was also the only bald pirate there; Benjamin Hornigold, who was a bit older than most, his hair having gone grey, and yet he still had that mad fire behind his eyes; Henry Morgan, who was a tall handsome man with a small moustache and beard more in that Spanish style; and the wide-eyed and somewhat innocent looking Stede Bonnet, who, if he hadn't been a pirate, looked as if he would have been more at home being an accountant.

The lights down by the stage were lit by a couple of the barmaids, as the other two snuffed out the lights around the walls. From behind a blue velvet curtain that had been draped at the rear of the hastily erected stage, appeared the host for the evening in his finest bright-red jacket with gold buttons and embroidered cuffs, Captain Kidd.

As he crossed over to the front of the stage, there was some polite applause and he waited for it to die down before he began, reading the prepared notes on the scroll before him, one of the serving girls rolling the parchment along as he finished each line.

'Good evening, Pirates and Privateers, and welcome to the sixteenth Bahamas Annual Pirate Testimonial Awards.' There was another round of applause. 'It's been a great year. Captain Ned Lowe has recorded his 70th ship taken and Captain Vane's old Quartermaster Calico Jack has at last become captain of his own ship.'

There was some more polite applause as Captain Kidd looked around the room. He cleared his throat and continued.

'So, without further ado, let's begin with the first category. Best swing from a pirate ship to a prize ship whilst at sea.'

A young girl walked across the stage with an envelope and handed it to Captain Kidd.

'And the nominations are.'

Behind him a sheet dropped down with a drawing of Black Bart on a rope swinging from his ship to another.

'Black Bart, taking The San Marie.'

There was a ripple of polite applause as Bart stood to acknowledge their praise. Then the picture was replaced with one of Henry Morgan swinging on a rope.

'Henry Morgan, taking The Abigail,' Captain Kidd continued, the applause growing again as Henry took a bow.

The image changed this time to Hornigold.

'And finally for this category, Ben Hornigold for taking Les Crois du Nord.'

They applauded Ben, as he took his bow. Then a nervous hush filled the room as Kidd opened the envelope. He smiled as he looked out over the audience and announced.

'And the winner is.... Black Bart.'

As they applauded him, Black Bart made his way up onto the stage and received a small trophy of a skull carved in wood from the girl, who kissed him on the cheek before he kissed her back on hers. Then, holding his trophy up for all to see, he headed back to his table and sat down.

13

The night drew on, as did all the drinking, and one by one the other categories were announced and still Woodes had yet to win a prize. But he remained quietly confident, secure in the knowledge that there was still one more be announced, the most prestigious prize of them all.

Captain Kidd rested his hands on the lectern and looked out over the crowd.

'And now to the last category of the night. Best Pirate Captain or Commander.'

There was a hushed murmur around the room.

Woodes turned to Pike.

'This is it. If I win this, I'll be the most famous pirate in the Caribbean.'

Captain Kidd waved the room to silence.

'Now,' he began, 'please show your appreciation for last year's winner of the award. Samuel Bellamy, best known to us as our loveable rogue, Black Sam.'

Black Sam quickly made his way up onto the stage and shook hands with Kidd as the rest applauded him.

'Thank you, Bill.' Sam grinned as he waved back to the crowd. A pretty young woman gave Sam the envelope and, as he crossed over to the lectern, Kidd standing a few feet back to give him room, Sam cleared his throat.

'And this year's nominations are.'

The sheet dropped to show an image of Stede Bonnet.

'Stede Bonnet.'

The audience applauded him as Stede took a bow, but Woodes wasn't worried by him. He might be brave, he sniffed, but he wasn't a very good captain and didn't even know the difference between a half-hitch and a sheepshank.

The image changed to show Jack Rackham.

'Calico Jack, Jack Rackham.' Sam announced to the audiences applause. Woodes sighed and rolled his eyes. Jack might be a good sailor and an excellent quartermaster, but as a captain, he couldn't be all that great. After all, his ship had the smallest crew in all of New Providence and one of them was a woman.

His confidence grew as the image changed to show himself.

'Woodes Rodgers.' Sam announced as the audience applauded heartily. He knew it was in the bag. Of the three, he was definitely the bravest.

'And finally,....' Woodes sat up and listened. He wasn't expecting that, '....Someone who's not a captain yet, but has moved up the ranks to quartermaster in just two years and the committee felt deserved to be included in this year's nominations.'

The sheet dropped to show none other than....

'Anne Bonny.' Sam cried, as the audience applauded. 'And now, the moment we've all been waiting for.' Sam opened the envelope. 'And I have to say, this goes to someone who so richly deserves it.'

Woodes' chest began to swell with pride.

'Brave, loyal, resourceful,' Sam continued, 'a very able seaman and skilled with both cutlass and flintlock.' He paused. 'The award goes to, none other than.... Anne Bonny.'

Woodes was devastated with shock. The audience applauded wildly. Anne waved to them all as she crossed to the stage, leapt up onto it and took the trophy from Sam. They shook hands and stood for a moment smiling as the artist quickly sketched them, then together they left the stage with the girl leading them off as Captain Kidd came over to the lectern.

'Now as another successful BAPTA's comes to a close, let us all charge our tankards and raise them in our traditional toast.'

There was a loud scraping of chairs and a bit of a muttering going on as everyone in the hall stood. Captain Kidd continued.

'To the money-grabbing, land-stealing tight-fisted, old harpy, squeezer of the poor and downright greedy old bitch. I give you. The Queen.' He held his tankard aloft. 'May she rot in hell.'

Everyone raised their tankards and cried,' To hell with the Queen.'

*

Back in his cabin, on The Duke, Woodes and Pike sat either side of his desk as Woodes poured out some rum for them both and they took a solemn drink.

'That prize should have been mine.' Woodes broke the silence and then drained and refilled his glass.

'You did deserve it, Captain,' Pike agreed.

'But instead it went to that Irish tart, Bonny. What she's got that I haven't got?'

Pike thought for a moment, then replied, 'A nice pair

of tits? A pert arse? She don't smell too bad either.'

'Yes, yes, but apart from all that! What makes her so different to the rest of us?'

They drained their glasses.

'A nice pair of tits, a pert arse and a nice smell!' Pike replied helpfully as Woodes refilled their glasses.

'Well, it won't do. She's made me look like I'm not a proper man.'

'I know she's a little butch, but I'm sure people will still know the difference,' Pike responded.

'It won't do, Pike.' He slammed the table. 'I must have my revenge on her. It's just not right, a woman robbing me of my chance to be the most famous pirate in history.'

They drank in silence.

'How, Captain?' Pike asked.

'How, indeed?'

14

It was a bright sunny day, not a cloud in the sky. On the busy quayside, Anne was checking the goods being loaded onto The Neptune as Pike and Woodes came over to her.

'Oi!' Woodes cried out to her. 'I want a word with you!'

She looked over to him as Dobbins stepped down the gangplank.

'Take over, will you, Dobbins?' she told him as she handed him the manifest.

'Aye, Ma'am,' He replied as she went over to Woodes and Pike.

'Well?'

'Not too bad, a slight headache,' Pike replied, rubbing his temple as Woodes slapped him on the shoulder.

'It's about that award you got yesterday.'

'What about it?' She shrugged.

'What gives you the right to muscle in on our business and take away our awards!' Woodes seethed. 'I mean, look at you. You're a woman! Shouldn't you be at home, cooking the dinner, instead of being out enjoying yourself all day?'

She grabbed him by his coat lapels.

'Now you listen to me, you sour-faced little turd!' she snarled. 'I won that award fair and square, and I don't need no ponced-up little shit-bag of a French fancy to tell me what I can and can't do. I'll rip your tiny dick up through your throat and stick it up your arse if you come around here telling me what I can and can't do again! Got it?'

She pushed him away and as he fell to the floor, she glared at Pike, who quickly backed away. Then kicking some dirt at Woodes, she turned on her heels and headed back to The Neptune as Pike helped him up to his feet.

'Well, you can't say fairer than that, Captain.' Pike shrugged as he dusted him down.

But Woodes wasn't prepared to let it lie there.

*

Later that day, Woodes and Pike headed down the narrow streets on their way to the inn.

'The thing is, Pike, we've been going about this all the wrong way.' He put his arm around Pike's shoulder. 'It's not Anne's fault she's so good at her job. It's because that arse Rackham's so bad.'

'I get you, Captain,' Pike agreed, 'but she's his quartermaster and she don't want to leave!'

'But if Rackham wasn't their captain anymore, then what?'

Woodes waited as Pike thought for a moment.

'Thing is....' They turned a corner and down a slight hill towards the inn, '....he is, and it's probably because he's the only man in all of New Providence who she'll listen to. I mean, Captain, she's a great quartermaster. That's why she won that award.'

Woodes slapped him around the head.

'But if he ain't captain, what happens?' he asked again.

'Well, they elect another, and then they elect the new roles as the captain proposes them.'

'And chances are,' Woodes began gleefully, 'she wouldn't be quartermaster under any other captain 'cos most of the guys here don't want no bossy woman doing their jobs better than they can as captain. So she'll be cast adrift shipless.'

'Not sure about that. She can really hold her liquor.'

'Shipless.' Woodes sighed.

'Oh.'

'Without a friend in the world. Just right then to join our crew and make The Duke the most famous ship ever in all history.'

Pike thought for a moment and then replied.

'Even more famous than The Queen Anne's Revenge or The Golden Hind? The Adventure Prize or The Sudden Death or The Ranger?'

'Most famous ship ever in all, all history.'

Pike was a little confused and asked.

'Yeah, but, Captain, how you going to discredit Rackham so his crew ditch him and Mistress Bonny?'

'I have an idea, Pike. You leave that to me. You just get our ship ready to sail.'

'Aye, Captain.' Pike grinned and ran back up the hill as Woodes entered the inn.

15

His eyes had to adjust for a moment to the darker surroundings, but as they did so, he could see that the inn was virtually empty, but for a few customers and those serving girls. The landlord was behind his counter. He spat into one of his tankards and wiped it out clean, placing it ready to one side for the next person to order an ale as Woodes looked around the room looking for someone to embroil in his scheme.

Stede Bonnet was sitting in a far corner all on his own, having lunch with his half tankard of drink and, after a moment to make sure no one from The Neptune's crew were about, Woodes went over to him and sat down opposite.

'Captain Bonnet.' Woodes spoke warmly.

'Captain Rodgers, to what do I owe this pleasure?'

'I was wondering, is it true, you're off to Florida on

the noon tide?'

'Sort of,' Stede replied, adding, 'we're planning to intercept The Lazy Jane out of Jamaica.'

'Oww.' Woodes sucked the air sharply over his teeth as he gently shook his head. 'Not sure I would if I was you.'

'No?' Stede asked, feeling a little concerned.

'No,' Woodes agreed. 'She's heavily armed. And, well, let's face it, you're not the best captain in the world, are you?'

'Well, no,' Stede agreed. 'Up until last year I owned a plantation growing sugar.'

'And now, bankrupt and a pirate.'

'True, but my crew love me.' Stede smiled appreciatively.

'They were your slaves!' Woodes sighed.

'And now they're my crew and one day, when we hit the big prize, I've promised them all their freedom to leave my employ.'

'Noble, I'm sure.' Woodes sighed. 'But look, Stede. I may call you Stede, may I?'

'You may.'

'The thing is, Stede, I don't think you and your men will have much joy with that ship. You'd be best letting some other crew take her and concentrate on smaller ships that trade around these islands.'

'You sure?' Stede asked nervously, not wishing to look weak amongst his fellow pirates.

'I'm sure.' Woodes nodded. 'If I was you, I'd give the info to that Bonny woman and let her crew do with it as they see fit. Trust me.' He smiled. 'I'm your friend.'

Woodes turned to the landlord and signalled he wanted two pints.

'I don't know.' Stede replied, reluctant to let such a large prize slip through his fingers. 'I mean, the guys really, they're looking for a big prize. Surely if we start tackling little ships, they're not going to get a big prize now, are they?'

'Yes, but you've got to work up to it,' Woodes advised him. 'Get them battle-ready, as it were.'

A serving girl arrived with their two tankards. She smiled sweetly at them both and curtsied before leaving them.

'And you say I should let Mistress Bonny have the details instead?' Stede asked. Woodes nodded. 'But it cost me two pounds that information.'

Woodes sighed and then took his wallet out of his coat pocket.

'Two pounds.' He placed the money on the table. 'And look. Here's two shillings. I'll pay for your meal and board. Do we have a deal?'

Bonnet thought for a moment and, with a reluctant sigh, he shook hands with Woodes.

'Oh, and just one other thing,' Woodes added. 'You couldn't make sure a letter I'm about to write goes on The Santa Barbara, could you? She's due in Port Royal this week. Do me a favour so I don't have to cross the quay like. Just give it to her captain. He'll make sure it gets to the right person.' And from his coat he took out a sheet of paper and signalled to the landlord.

'Landlord. Could I have a pen, ink and sealing wax?'

The landlord sighed and rolled his eyes.

*

As Woodes left the inn and headed up the hill, from the direction of the harbour, Anne and Jack came along and went inside.

*

As Jack went up to the counter to get the drinks, Anne found a nice table, not too near the door. Bonnet watched her. He had now finished his lunch and after draining his drink he crossed over to her table.

'Mistress Bonny.'

'Captain Bonnet,' she replied courteously.

'Anne.' Stede sat beside her. 'I was wondering if you would do me the pleasure.' He glanced around the room.

'If you want any of that, see the girls next door,' she replied.

'Oh, no, look, you misunderstand,' he reassured her, glancing around the room again. 'You see I've got this information about a prize heading for Florida, but it's a bit too big for me. My crew don't have much experience and we wondered, you being a BAPTA winner, if you'd like to have first crack at it.'

She waved for him to give her the details, which he duly did, taking care not to give her the letter as well. She looked at it.

'A colonial brigantine.' She smirked, her eyes lighting up as she could see it was a prize worth taking. He nodded as she continued. 'Thanks, Bonnet, we'll make sure this info's put to good use.'

He smiled and left the inn as Jack crossed to the table carrying the two frothing tankards of ale.

'You alright there, my lover?' he asked. 'Not bothering you, was he?'

'No.' She spread the page on to the table. 'He's just given us this.' Anne took her beer as he looked at the paper and read it carefully.

'Problem is Anne, my sweet,' he sighed. 'We've promised the boys a run down to Saint Kitts. We can't start heading north as well.' He took a sip of ale. 'We took a vote and, you know, it's sort of agreed.'

'Shame to waste it.' She took a large slurp of her ale as Jack nodded in agreement. Then an idea struck him.

'Give it to Black Bart. He likes the colonials.'

*

Anne met up with Captain Black Bart on the quarterdeck of The Fortune, just as Bart was readying his own ship to set sail.

She waited as Black Bart carefully read the paper.

'Sure. Why not?' He shrugged. 'We're not doing anyone specific at the moment. We'll have a crack at it.'

'Cheers, Bart.' She kissed him on the cheek. 'Buy Jack and me a pint when you get back.'

'Will do,' he agreed.

He watched her carefully as she left the ship, then waited as his Quartermaster Coates came up the steps to him. He read the paper again.

'Captain.' Coates began excitedly. 'That ship we're after, our source says she's heading for the Bahamas, south of Cuba, so we should be able to take her at Rum island.'

'Damn, and she's a full brig.' Bart swore. 'Look, we can't take them both.' He slapped the paper as Coates took a look at it and understood why. The Lazy Jane was going to be too far north. 'Take this over to Captain Morgan. He's always up for a bit of fun.'

*

Coates found Captain Henry Morgan up on the quarterdeck of his ship, The Satisfaction, overseeing some minor repairs to the bulwark where it had rotted over the years. There he read the page as Coates waited patiently.

'It's a worthy prize, I agree.' Morgan was impressed. 'But you must remind Black Bart, I'm a privateer. I'm only allowed to attack Spanish ships. This is a colonial ship, out of Virginia. I can't take her, or else in Port Royal they'll cut my privileges off.'

Coates winced. No man likes to have his privileges cut off. Morgan folded the page back in half as he thought carefully for a moment.

'Try Lowe,' he suggested, adding, 'he'll attack anything he can stick his blade into and he's looking for a new ship.

his current, The Pink Rose, needs a lot of repair, so he'll probably jump at the chance of taking her.'

*

On the quarterdeck of The Pink Rose, Coates watched as Captain Ed Lowe, whilst leaning against his ship's wheel, carefully read the paper.

'Thing is,' he said folding the paper and handing it back to Coates, 'until my repairs are complete, I can't sail, not for another week. Pity, only my blades are rusting without a bit of blood to keep them slippery.' He looked back across the bay as he thought hard for a moment. 'Tell you what.' He turned back to Coates. 'I know who is desperate for a prize, especially after that humiliation he suffered at the awards.'

'Who?' Coates asked.

'Well, it won't be Jack, will it? He's already pussy whipped and Bonnet's a novice of the worst kind. No, that stuck up shit, what's his name?'

'Captain Rodgers you mean?' asked Coates.

'Aye.' Lowe nodded. 'Give it to his quartermaster, Pike. Tell him it's from me and I'm sure they'll use it.'

16

Two days later, out in the Caribbean sea, The Duke was at full sail with the wind nicely behind her, travelling at almost her full speed, high in the water, her cargo hold still to be filled.

On her quarterdeck, the helm kept them on an even course. Woodes and Pike watched over the main deck as their crew busied themselves.

Woodes took his telescope and then, moving over to the bulwark, looking out over the sea.

'You sure this is the right place, Pike?'

'Sure am, Captain,' Pike replied, 'Got the details from Black Bart's quartermaster, and he got them from Captain Lowe himself, he says.'

'So we know they're genuine.'

'Ship ahoy,' a voice called down from the top of the mainmast, 'Off the starboard bow.'

Woodes and Pike looked, through their telescopes to the ship's right-hand side.

'Turn fifteen degrees to starboard, Mr Key,' Woodes ordered his helm. 'Once we're running at full speed, have them raise the black flag, Mr Pike.'

'Aye, Captain.'

'A brigantine, and she's very heavy in the water. She'll make a nice prize.' Woodes smiled with proud self-satisfaction, as in his mind he began to spend his money on those important things, gambling, women and rum.

'She's The Lazy Jane, sir, carrying mostly rum and sugar out of Jamaica,' Pike informed him and suddenly Woodes turned pale.

'The Lazy Jane?' he nervously asked.

'Aye, Captain,' Pike confirmed and then he asked. 'Why? Something the matter?'

'Oh, no. As you were.'

*

The Duke closed on The Lazy Jane. She was only yards away from her stern, when suddenly, as if from out of nowhere, another ship, an English frigate, slipped out from her shadow and dropped back a few yards until she was level with The Duke.

*

'Frigate!!' shouted Pike.
'Just what I was thinking,' Woodes agreed.

*

Before The Duke could do anything, before an order could be given, the frigate opened up and gave The Duke a full broadside.

ANTHONY DAY

*

In the large market square in the centre of Hamilton, Bermuda's capital city, and just in front of the governor's mansion, Woodes Rodgers and two other government officials, each in their long coats, white britches and stockings and long, white, powdered wigs, stood at the front of a baying crowd as they watched the execution of Pike and the last of The Duke's crew.

There was the sudden scraping of the stools as the executioner kicked them away one by one and the taut sound of the ropes as they tightened around the men's necks. They kicked, choked and squirmed as they died, the crowd cheering, laughing and teasing them for being pussies.

'Now that you've had all your crew hung and have renounced piracy, have you decided what you want to do?' the first official asked as he and the second began to lead Woodes away.

'Well....' Woodes shrugged. 'I can't go back to England yet, and I do love it here in the Caribbean. I was wondering if there was a position somewhere here I could take up?'

'Well,' the first official began thoughtfully. 'We do need an administrator here. The new King wants to expand business in the Caribbean, and we need someone to oversee the shipments as they come and go.'

'If you're good at that,' the second official added, 'who knows, in a couple of years' time, you could be governor of Jamaica.'

They both laughed as Woodes thought about that for a moment.

'Could I?' he asked.

'Don't see why not,' the first official agreed. 'If you marry the right girl, that is.'

'And we know just the right girl, don't we, Clive?' the other teased.

'She a right girl, that's right, Rupert.' The first official agreed. They both put their arms around Woodes and led him away to a nearby tavern to discuss his future prospects in more detail.

*

Suddenly, the door flew open. He looked up and there, large in the doorway, Mrs Rodgers stood. She shouted, 'And another thing. The wallpaper in our quarters.'

He put the black cloth away, closing the drawer firmly as he turned his attention to her.

'What's wrong with it, my precious?'

'It's too yellow!' she cried. 'I hate yellow stripes.'

'What do you suggest, the sweetness of my life?' he asked.

'Green,' she replied. 'Yes, green. No, pink. Pink or green. Anything but yellow.'

'Right you are, my sweet. I will have the servants find us some ship heading back to England or to New York and place an order for some green or some pink wallpaper immediately.'

'I should think so.' She huffed and stormed out, slamming the door.

'Damn women and damn that Anne Bonny for ruining my life.'

He slammed the top of his desk hard.

17

A light breeze was coming of the harbour and the markets of Nassau were alive with the business of the day.

The light sprightly step of boots echoed down the gangplank of the merchantman as Mary Read took her first steps onto dry land for several months. She was dressed as a man, wearing an old, battered, tri-corn hat, a long, blue, Dutch cavalry coat, trousers and boots. She had an angelic, soft, boyish face and was skinny like a boy. She even went by the name of Mark as it was Mary's secret she was a woman.

In truth, she had spent almost all her life, since the age of five, living like a boy or a man, so being a man was really all she knew and New Providence wasn't going to be anywhere different. As far as they and anyone would ever know, she was a man.

She took a long look along the quay. Then seeing an

inn on the corner of the street facing onto the docks, she slung her small kitbag over her shoulder and made her way over to it.

*

The large room of the inn was busy with sailors drinking and some eating, but it wasn't crowded. Mary made her way to the far end where the landlord stood behind his counter filling a pint tankard from one of the large barrels for a serving girl to take away.

She waited until the landlord turned to her. 'What can I get you, squire?' he asked.

'Ale, landlord,' she replied, finding a coin from her jacket. 'You know if anyone's hiring?'

The landlord brought her drink over to her, some of the froth dribbling over the side as he placed the tankard down on the counter. He thought hard for a moment.

'Have you experience?' he asked wryly as she handed him the coin.

'Three years with the British Navy before I joined the army.'

'Isn't that a Dutch cavalry jacket?' he asked, nodding to her coat.

'Blue goes better with my eyes.' She smiled. 'And I don't like walking.'

The landlord gave her a strange look up and down as he thought for a moment.

'You could try The Neptune,' he suggested with a quick shrug. 'She's always looking for crew.'

'Is she a good ship?' Mary asked.

'Oh yes, only... ' He glanced around making sure no one was listening to them and leant over to her across the counter. 'She's cursed.' He spoke with a hushed voice.

'Cursed?' she asked nervously.

'On account of her quartermaster being....' He glanced both ways. 'I can't say.'

The old man in the corner smoking a pipe sat up.

'She be cursed alright!' he called out to Mary. 'Take it from me. I was a young man just like yourself, until I served on that cursed ship! Now look at me, six months at sea and reduced to a quivering wreck.'

'How?' Mary asked. 'What's so terrible about The Neptune?'

A murmur rippled around the inn.

'Buy me an ale, young man, and I'll tell you,' the old man called back, pointing his pipe at Mary.

She put a coin on the bar. The landlord poured the pint and gave the tankard to a serving girl who took it over to the old man.

The old man took a long sup of his ale. Then after wiping his lips with the back of his sleeve, he turned to Mary, beckoning her to listen.

'It's the most terrifying experience on all this earth,' he continued. 'I've seen swells so high, higher than the mizzen mast, that they could swallow a ship in one; creatures so strange but with such sweet voices they could lure a man to his doom, wrecking his ship on the rocks; sea serpents so huge that they could crush a ship in their jaws, but nothing, nothing so terrible as that of the curse of The Neptune.' He drained his tankard dry as Mary waited with bated breath. The old man paused and wiped the last of the drink from his lips. 'The Neptune's quartermaster.' He shook his head, the terror of it welling in his eyes. 'It's too terrible to say.'

'Try?' Mary encouraged him. 'Is it Welsh? I know it's always very difficult to get all those rolling vowel sounds.'

'No, it's not Welsh, it's... it's....' The whole room leant in to listen to him. 'The quartermaster's a woman.'

There were gasps. The serving girls shrieked with shock and one of them fainted. Mary was the only one not to react, just smiling devilishly to herself, as instead she shrugged and drank her ale.

'And what's so terrible about that?' she asked the old

man. 'We live in exciting times. We're no longer slaves to our past traditions. Why shouldn't a woman be in charge of a ship? Why not one day have a woman as captain?'

The whole inn gasped and the same serving girl fainted yet again.

'It may sound fun to you, my young lad,' the old man continued earnestly. 'But when I went to sea, we never had a woman on board. It was bad luck. Ships have a habit of sinking and getting lost as it is, never mind adding bad luck to the mix. Now when I went to sea, we were all hard men. Our boats were full of seamen, tossed together in them, our tiny vessels out to discover the new promised lands. Take my word for it, young lad. If you mix women and seamen together, you get nothing but trouble.'

The inn turned quiet. Mary sipped her ale as she thought for a moment. She turned to the landlord.

'So, where can I find her?' she smiled and sipped her drink.

'Wait here long enough.' The landlord checked his watch. 'I'm sure they'll find you.'

18

The inn doors were flung open and in came Anne Bonny. The other drinkers quickly shied away from her as she passed them by and strolled up to the counter.

'It's been a hard day, landlord.' She slapped the counter with the flat of her hand. 'Give me your strongest liquor.'

She looked over the drinkers cowering behind their tankards trying not to look in her direction. When she turned back to the bar, the landlord was holding one of his serving girls by the arm and pushed her over to Anne.

'No, I need some rum.' Anne sighed as she looked the girl up and down. 'Well... maybe later.'

With a meek, smile the serving girl curtsied and left.

'Right you are, Mistress Bonny,' the landlord replied, as he took a bottle of rum from a shelf next to his barrels. Pulling the loose cork out with his teeth, he poured as

Anne looked around the room. He placed the glass in front of her as she turned to him, putting a coin down on the counter. The landlord picked it and Anne turned back to face the room.

'I'm looking for crew,' she announced and then downed her drink in one. When she looked back to the room, the bar was empty, but for Mary still standing at the other end of the counter.

'Crew, you say?' Mary asked.

'That's right.' Anne turned to her. 'I run a tight ship. She's an armed sloop, a privateer and the best in all of New Providence.'

'Unless you count William Teach, Captain Kidd, Charles Vane....' She cut the landlord off mid-sentence with the raising of a hand.

'The best,' she stressed.

'Well... I am looking to go to sea, ' Mary replied.

'Then join our crew and I promise you I'll show you a good time.' Mary paused to think as Anne added, 'And if the winds favourable, we might get some sailing in too.' She waited as Mary sipped her ale. 'So? What do you say?'

*

Jack and Dobbins were by the main mast, checking the rigging, when Mary and Anne arrived on the deck.

'The repairs are done?' Jack asked.

'Aye, Captain, but I cannot tell you how well they'll fare in bad weather.'

'I'm sure they'll be fine. Didn't our carpenter, Howell over see the work?'

'When he was sober, aye.'

'Calico,' Anne interrupted. Jack and Dobbins turned to her and saw Mary.

'Anne, who's this?' Jack asked, pointing to Mary.

'A potential new recruit.'

'And who would you be, young lad?' Jack asked.

'Mark Read.' Mary replied.

'Well, young Mister Read, today's your lucky day.' Dobbins, listening, rolled his eyes to the sky as Jack continued. 'As it so happens, there is vacancy for membership of my crew. I won't pretend to you that life aboard will lack adventure. But to every man who joins me, I can promise you for your troubles, each ordinary seaman shall receive a single share. On average, my friend, you will earn a year's wage in just one share. And I don't mean the mega wage they give you on a merchantman, but compared to the Royal Navy, if this was a man-o-war, you would be getting, before stoppages, only 19 shillings per month and with me, no stoppages and a year's wage. That's eleven pounds at least. Not bad for a bunch of rogues eh? So, lad? Will you sign with me?'

'I will.'

'Good lad. Master Dobbins, the book.'

'Are you sure you want to do that, Captain?' Dobbins asked. 'It will mean sharpening another nib.'

'Of course, Master Dobbins,' Jack replied. 'We may be unprincipled scum, lawless and rogues, every man jack. But we must do these things proper like.'

Dobbins rolled his eyes with a heavy sigh.

'Nothing good will come of it, Captain.'

'Go get the book before I box your ears!' Anne snapped and Dobbins seemed a little scared of her,

'Yes, Ma'am.' he replied, before quickly heading off down below to get the book.

'You will like it here, boy.' Jack put his arm around Mary and led her a little further along the ship towards the helm as Anne followed a yard or so behind, giving Mary the once-over.

'I'm sure I will, Captain.' Mary replied with an angelic smile.

'Our Mistress Bonny will take you through your duties.' Jack explained as they passed Bourn coiling some rope. 'She's our first mate.'

'Constantly.' Bourn muttered under his breath and as Anne walked past, she punched him knocking him out as they all continued towards the quarterdeck.

'Our Quartermaster.' Jack continued. 'We maintain a portion of our bounty in a central fund to compensate for injuries one might sustain. From our fund, for example, 600 pieces of eight will be paid for the loss of a leg, 100 pieces for loss of an eye. We are an equal opportunities employer, as you can see. Even ex-slaves are welcome and, before we set sail, we all have a simple hands-up vote on who will be captain and the other roles and at any time anyone can challenge for a role if they feel they would be better suited, but should you lose the ship's confidence, it's the custom to set the loser adrift in a rowing boat with one week's provisions.'

Mary smiled. 'Sounds fair.'

Dobbins came back to Jack and Mary carrying the book, which he quickly held open, the page already marked with the pen dividing the pages.

'If you'll make your mark there, my lad.' Jack pointed to the first empty line as Dobbins carefully placed the book down on a barrel with the portable inkwell next to it. Mary took the pen, dipped it in the ink and wrote her name in a beautiful rolling script that impressed both Jack and Anne, who were looking over Mary's shoulder.

'You've been well educated, Mister Read.' Jack commented, looking at the page as Mary stepped away, putting the pen down.

'I had a good enough childhood, Captain,' she replied.

Anne sniffed Mary's hair as she moved away and came around Mary to stand beside her. Jack handed Dobbins the book and he gathered up the inkwell, taking it all back down below.

'All that's left to say is welcome aboard,' Jack continued. 'Now I must check provisions so I'll leave you in Mistress Bonny's capable hands.'

He walked away leaving them alone, standing by the

wheel.

'We concentrate on smaller vessels and Dutch flutes, chiefly,' Anne began as Mary turned to her. 'We never harm a crew that surrenders though it doesn't hurt to make them think we will if they don't but I'll never lead you onto a vessel I don't think we can take. Concentrate first on food, water, alcohol, weapons, clothing, soap, rope and anchors. We can sell them easy anywhere, not just in New Providence, but diamonds, jewels we don't touch. Gold however, that and silver are another matter, but you won't find much of that. That's your brigantines'.' Anne slapped the wheel. 'Our vessel be a bit small to take on one of them in open water. Medicines are, however, a must. If the ship has a medical chest, take it. We get from £300 to £400 for one of them alone.'

'What?' Mary began to do the maths. 'That's,1 piece of eight is worth 4s 3d in New Providence. That's just over four pieces of eight to the pound. That's over fifteen hundred pieces of eight. My quarters in town were only two pieces of eight for the month!'

'But that's only if you find the chest,' Anne reminded her. 'Some of these merchants hide it so well, we'd be back in Bristol before we found it.'

They looked out to sea and as Mary watched the horizon, Anne quickly took an admiring look at Mary's bottom.

'How long have you sailed under the captain?' Mary asked.

'Three year. In fact, I should say, he's only been captain a year. He was originally the quartermaster and I was his secret lover on The Revenge.' Mary watched Anne as she crossed to the bulwark and sat down. 'I was on the run from my husband, the worst, no-good, two-timing slime to have ever crawled out of Satan's arse. James Bonny.' Mary sat down beside Anne. 'But I left that no-good lump of excrement and hooked up with Jack. He suggested I should pretend to be a man so we could join his ship under her previous captain. Charles Vane. But he chickened out on us taking a French man-o-war. So, we took a vote, and Vane and his supporters lost.'

'What happened then?' Mary asked.

'They were put in a rowing boat with a week's provisions and set to sea.'

'And did he?' Mary turned to look to the sea again.

'He did.'

Mary took her hat off in respect.

'Not sure he's ever really forgiven us,' Anne added.

'He survived then?' Mary was surprised.

'We were only a mile out from the shore. I mean, we're not bad people really. Just a little bit misunderstood.'

Mary smiled as Anne looked into her eyes and, for a moment as they held the gaze, they both felt like a pair of teenage lovers, before they suddenly shook themselves from each other's stare and glanced away a little embarrassed.

'And Calico's been our captain ever since,' Anne concluded looking back down the boat to see if she could see where he was.

'Calico?' Mary asked, puzzled, as Anne stood up.

'Aye, our nickname for him, 'cos he wears those calico trousers.'

Mary stood up as Anne put her arm around her shoulder. They walked back to the main deck passing Carty who was greasing the helm.

'Don't worry your pretty little face about anything,' Anne assured her. 'You have a problem, you come to me. That's what I'm here for. Day or night. I'll be able to fit you in.'

'She'll do that all right,' Carty teased, only for Anne to punch and knock him out.

'Thank you.' Mary smiled warmly. 'Already I feel so at home.'

19

The Neptune was at full sail heading away from the sun. The wind was filling her sails as it cut across the ship, and she was high in the water, travelling almost at full speed.

On the quarterdeck, Anne was standing next to Davis at the helm. In front of them on the main deck, all the other crewmembers except for Calico were working, either swabbing down the deck or coiling ropes. When she saw her, Mary was coiling some rope.

Anne walked a few paces towards the rail to watch Mary for a while.

'What you think of that young fellow?'

'Which one?' Davis asked looking away from the sea to the main deck as Anne turned to face him.

'The new lad.'

'Mark?' he asked.

'Aye him. There's a stud if there ever was one.'

'Don't let Calico hear yah,' he warned her. 'You know he gets jealous of your messing around with the crew.'

'Like I care!' She sniffed. 'He's not my husband.'

'No, but that's only 'cos you're married already,' Davis reminded her. 'Jack may be a scoundrel, a cheat and a villainous rogue but deep down, he's a pretty honest guy!'

'Just you hold a steady course. South by south-west.'

He checked his compass.

'We're on course,' he replied.

'You make sure of that.'

She then began to walk down to the deck as Earl, carrying a bucket, came up the steps, walked past Davis and was about to throw the water overboard, when Davis stopped him.

'Tom?'

'What?' Earl came over to him.

'What's the compass say?'

Thomas took a look.

'South by south-east.'

'Where's south by south-west?'

Earl pointed on the compass where it was and Davis started to turn the wheel so that the arrow pointed to the right setting. The floating plate that was marked up as the compass bounced and rocked while it moved as the ship began to move to the new direction.

Anne looked up to the sky as she noticed the ship was changing course, but then shrugged and continued doing her rounds.

Earl watched as Davis turned the ship. The wind started to come across from a different angle and the sails rippled overhead. As Davis started to hold the boat on its new steady course, Earl slapped him lightly across the arm.

'Now you're heading the right way. Keep the arrow pointing there, you can't go wrong.' He then headed to the back of the ship and, as he threw the bucket of water out to sea, the wind caught it and threw it back, soaking him.

'I see, so now we've the wind behind us.'

Jack and Dobbins arrived on the quarterdeck as Earl passed them on his way back to the steps.

'Earl,' Jack said. 'Don't you know, you're supposed to keep the wind on your back when you throw the waste overboard.'

'Aye, Cap'n,' Earl replied continuing down the ship to his duties. Jack held out his hand and Dobbins gave him the large telescope.

'How long have we been out of New Providence?'

'A week, Captain,' Dobbins replied.

'And you're sure we're near to the Cuban trail?'

'No, sir.'

'No, Dobbins?' Jack turned to him.

'Not until we sight a merchantman, sir, no, Captain.' Jack shrugged then looked out to sea as Dobbins added, 'What I do know, sir, is we should be in the right place by now.'

'Good.'

Dobbins took the telescope as he and Jack crossed over to Davis. Jack looked out over the main deck and saw Anne crossing over to Mary. He watched them for a while as they talked happily to one another.

'I see Mistress Bonny's spending more time with our newbie.'

'She spends a lot of time with the newbie,' Dobbins remarked. Jack turned to him.

'You don't think she spends too much time with him, do you?'

'Of course not, Captain,' Dobbins lied, adding, 'I mean, she swore she would never have another affair with another man after you and she took command of this vessel. You gave her that ultimatum. It was you or Captain Vane, and she chose you, Captain, on the grounds that you helped her escape that arse of a husband of hers.'

'True.' Jack agreed.

'Though of course,' Dobbins continued, 'when she

pledged herself to you like that, young Mister Read wasn't on our ship, now was he, Captain?'

'No, he wasn't.' Jack admitted uneasily and suddenly he began to resent her talking to the new young man.

'And he is a handsome-looking man,' Dobbins pointed out, 'so fresh of face with a lovely smile. You know, if I was a fudge packer, which I'm not, I could quite fancy the bloke myself!'

'I see what you mean.' Jack thought hard for a moment. 'And you think my Anne might have noticed this Mister Read's good looks and gentle charms herself?'

'Now you know I'm not one to gossip, sir,' Dobbins explained, 'but, as you can see, she does spend a lot of time talking to the young fellow.'

Mary had nearly finished her coiling of the rope. Anne was still talking to her and Jack's blood was beginning to simmer.

'Dobbins, come with me.' And together they marched down the deck towards Anne and Mary.

20

'You're a fine worker, Mark, me lad,' Anne gushed, 'but there are still some things I'd like to know about you.'

'Sure, anything you want to know, Ma'am.'

Anne looked up and could see Jack approaching. Suddenly she became a bit nervous and all self-conscious.

'I think maybe we should like to talk, later.'

'Talk?' Mary asked.

'I'll put you on late watch tonight. We can talk then.'

Before Mary could answer her, Jack and Dobbins joined them.

'Mistress Bonny.'

'Calico.'

'Don't you think we should have a lookout topside?' He pointed to the top of the mainmast.

Anne looked out to sea and then back to Jack.

'Think you're right. I'll just find someone to....'

But Jack interrupted her. 'Why not young Mark here. You've climbed to the nest before now, haven't you, lad?'

'Aye, Captain,' Mary replied.

'Then up you go. That is, if you don't mind, Mistress Bonny.'

'No, of course not, Captain.'

Mary noticed there seemed to be a tension between them both, but shrugging it off, she started to climb the rigging to the top of the mainmast.

'If you don't need me any longer, Captain,' Dobbins continued, 'I'll just go and see if Master Fenwick has finished readying the cannon.'

'You do that, Master Dobbins.'

Dobbins left them.

'I was just telling the newbie about how brave and daring you are,' Anne remarked, lightly touching Jack upon his chest as she lowered her head and fluttered her long eyelashes at him.

'You were?' He was surprised and flattered.

'Nothing more.' She promised, leaving her hand resting on his chest. 'You know you are the world to me, Jack. Why do you get so jealous?'

'Anne,' he sighed softly. 'If I ever thought I was going to lose you, I'm not sure how I could cope. You know, I have given up my friends, taken this boat, run a crew, everything, just for you.'

'I know.' And she kissed him gently upon the cheek.

'Promise me you'll never have an affair with another man.'

'I promise you.' She crossed her heart. 'On my life, I will never have an affair with another man, although, that doesn't mean we can't see other people, does it, Jack?'

'Of course not, my precious. I just want to make sure that, no matter what happens, you are only loyal to me. No other man will ever come between us.'

She nodded and after he kissed her tenderly on her lips, he walked away.

21

That night, under the light of a lantern, Mary was keeping watch at the front of the ship. She was tired and as she yawned, she stretched and then scratched her left armpit, before she yawned again and looked out once more to the vast blackness of the empty Caribbean sea.

From out of the hold's main hatch, Anne emerged. Checking she had not been seen by anyone else, or the other watch, she quickly and quietly made her way over to Mary.

'Ahoy there, young Mark,' she whispered as Mary turned to see her.

'Ma'am.'

They gazed into each other's eyes.

'You wanted to talk?' Mary asked.

'Talk?' For a moment Anne was confused and then she remembered her excuse. 'Oh yes, talk.'

They stood for a moment in silence as Anne looked her up and down.

'That coat you wear, it suits you,' she remarked.

'Thank you. It's an old Dutch cavalry coat.'

'Are you Dutch?' Anne asked as they both sat upon the bulwark.

'No, English,' Mary admitted. 'But I was in Flanders during the war.'

'So why aren't you with the Dutch army now?' Anne asked.

'The war ended and as I'd been to sea before, I thought why not.' Mary shrugged. 'I went first on a couple of merchantmen, but I missed the adventure and also, I wanted to make some money.'

'When we reach port, you must tell me all your stories. You must have had an interesting life,' Anne flattered her, wiping a hair away from Mary's forehead.

There they sat for a couple of moments just staring into each other's eyes.

'I was wondering?' Anne asked.

'Yes?'

'Have you a sweetheart back home?'

Mary gave Anne a wry smile. 'There has been no one special these past four years.'

'Pity,' Anne remarked, adding, 'such a handsome man as yourself, like, should be all alone in this world. It will not do, sure it won't.'

'You think me handsome?'

'Of course,' Anne assured her. 'You must have women falling at your feet.'

Mary blushed and looked away.

'You do like women?' Anne asked. 'I mean, you're not a French fancy, are you? I mean, it would be such a waste if you were.'

'Oh, no, no, I do like girls,' Mary replied. 'In fact, from my days in the Royal Navy as a powder monkey right through to the day I left The Netherlands, there's nothing

I have enjoyed more than the company of a girl, Ma'am.'

'I'm glad to hear it,' Anne replied relieved. 'Only we can spend a month at a time at sea, and it can be so lonely without the company of a fit, strong, handsome young man.'

She went to kiss Mary but Mary shied away.

'What is it?'

'The lads tell me you and Calico are like man and wife,' Mary replied.

'Don't you be worrying about Calico.' Anne grinned. 'He knows his place with me.' Mary returned the smile with one similar, which made Anne's smile all the broader. Then Anne moved closer for a kiss but yet again Mary stopped her.

'Ma'am, I must warn you. I'm not like other men.'

'You mean, you are a French fancy after all?' Anne's heart sank.

'No! I'm just not the man you think I am,' Mary replied.

'You're not a Bible thumper, are you?'

'No.'

'Then, Mark, my lad.' Anne took Mary by her hands. 'What's the problem? Since that first day you came aboard our boat, I have been intoxicated with you. You are the first thing I think of when the morning light wakes me and the last thing I think of when my hammock bumps into Jack's. You are my moon that lights my night-time dreams, the stars that navigate to my heart. You are the very breath I breathe. I had never been so hopelessly, head-over-hills in love with any man in all my life until you came along and showed me that there is joy to be had in being in love. I would walk on hot coals for you, fight duels for you and even crap on the bed of King George himself if I could guarantee just one kind word from your wonderful manly lips.'

'Thank you.' Mary smiled.

'I love you, Mark, like no woman has loved any

other.'

'Thanks again,' Mary replied. 'And in my heart I must confess I feel those things too. It's only I should...' But before Mary could say anything else, Anne kissed her passionately and as they kissed, Anne slipped her hand into Mary's trousers.

Suddenly they stop kissing and Anne quickly sat back, but kept her hand in Mary's trousers.

'You're a girl?'

'Of course I am. After all, it would be a funny place to keep a hairbrush!'

Anne was dumbstruck.

'But you're a girl?' was all she could say.

'When I was five,' Mary explained, 'my father died and my grandmother would only help support my mother and me if she had, had a son. So she dressed me as a boy and I was taught to be a boy and for all my life I have lived as a boy. I was a boy in the Royal Navy, and I fought for both the British and Dutch armies as a boy. I've always been a boy, but for one thing.'

'So I've noticed!' Anne admitted.

'You won't give me away, will you, Ma'am?' Mary pleaded. 'They say it's bad luck to have a woman on board a ship, and two on one vessel would make this the unluckiest ship on the high seas.'

'Don't worry,' Anne assured her. 'I shall keep your secret safe.'

'Suppose now you know, all those things you said, you wish to take back?'

'No.' Anne shook her head. 'I cannot shake these feelings I have for you, Mark. I mean, what is your true name?'

'Mary.'

'Mary. I like that name.' Anne repeated her name a couple of times in a soft whisper. 'I am in love with you with all my heart.'

'Even though I'm a woman?' Mary asked.

'Well... nobody's perfect,' Anne admitted.

They grinned at each other. Then, as Anne removed her hand from Mary's trousers, they kissed more passionately than before and they started to sink down amongst the ropes.

TO BE CONTINUED.......

ABOUT THE AUTHOR

Anthony Day was born in Margate, Kent and now lives in Whitstable writing contemporary, science fiction, fantasy and historically based fiction.

OTHER BOOKS BY THIS AUTHOR INCLUDE

MUNCH

Novella about a monster terrorizing Canterbury suitable for years 9+

THE ADVENTURES OF SAMANTHA BISHOP

Book series set in the 1920's. Following the adventures of two flappers who solve crimes and fight injustice. Suitable for young adults+

WAITING FOR A TRAIN

Ruth Holland finds herself stranded at a railway station were unless she can stop a train, she will die.

www.ingramcontent.com/pod-product-compliance
Lightning Source LLC
Chambersburg PA
CBHW071318040426
42444CB00009B/2047